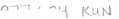

Izzie

Growing Up on the Plains in the 1880s

Text & Illustrations

by

Marion S. Kundiger & Jerri Garretson

Ravenstone Press

Manhattan, Kansas

1998

Dedicated to
Jeanette Isabella Caroline Anderson Swenson
whose stories of her childhood still charm after more than a century.

Cataloging Data from the publisher.
[This is not Library of Congress Cataloging in Publication (CIP) data.]

Kundiger, Marion S.
Garretson, Jerri.

Izzie: Growing up on the Plains in the 1880s / Marion S. Kundiger & Jerri Garretson ;
1st ed.

Summary: Thirteen episodes in the life of Isabella Anderson show what a child's life
was like in Fergus Falls, Minnesota during the late 1880s.

ISBN 0-9659712-1-X (paperbound)

[1. Swenson, Isabella Anderson, 1878 - 1952 - Biography.   2. Minnesota -- History.
3. Fergus Falls, Minnesota -- History.   4. Frontier and pioneer life -- Minnesota. 5.
Norwegian Americans -- Minnesota -- History.] I. Garretson, Jerri. II. Title.
977.604   1998

Printed in Manhattan, Kansas by Ag Press.

This book was typset in New Century Schoolbook using Word Perfect on a Macintosh
Performa.

Ravenstone Press, P.O. Box 1791, Manhattan KS 66505-1791   Tel: (785) 776-0556

Izzie

A Child's Life in the 1880s

Izzie's Stories

Isabella

(or "Izzie" for short)

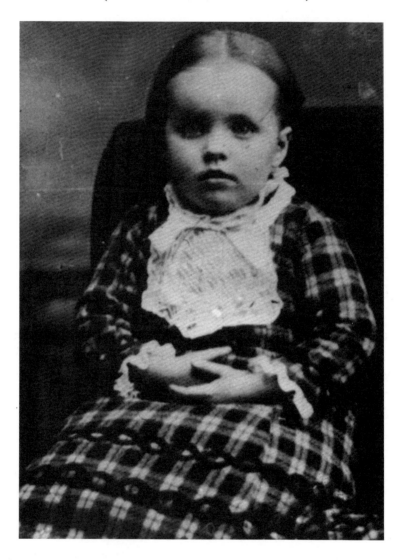

This is Izzie when she was about four years old around 1882. Her full name was Jeanette Isabella Caroline Anderson. She was born on September 24, 1878 in Fergus Falls, Minnesota.

In those days, there were no modern cameras. All photos were black and white. She had to hold very still for a long time to get her picture taken. That's why she looks stiff and isn't smiling. Izzie said all the old photos made them look solemn but kids were just as full of fun then as they are now.

Meet Izzie, Tightrope Walker

If you could travel back in time to the 1880s, you wouldn't find any television. There would be no radios, no video games, no malls, and no Barbie dolls. No one had heard of a videotape or a CD. What would you do for fun?

Izzie and her friends would show you how to have a good time. She was a tomboy who had to wear dresses, wool stockings, and high-top shoes fastened with long rows of tiny buttons because all girls had to dress like that in those days. That didn't stop her from playing in the hayloft, sledding, swinging, and climbing trees. It did mean she often came home dirty with holes in her clothes.

Isabella Anderson was born in 1878 in Fergus Falls, Minnesota. Everyone called her "Izzie." Izzie loved to have fun. One day she was running through a shortcut back of the Grand Hotel when she found a box of pink face powder. It must have fallen out one of the hotel windows. Makeup! Now she and her friends could get all powdered up and have a circus in her friend Alfred's barn.

Izzie's high-top, buttoned shoes.

The Grand Hotel

Izzie got all her friends together and fixed up the barn. She wanted to be a tightrope walker, so they fastened a rope across the barn and she performed on that. It was hard to balance but it didn't hurt when she fell off in the hay.

They put up a trapeze, too, and did tricks on it. Izzie was certainly not very ladylike hanging upside down with her bloomers showing but she had a great time!

They pretended that their dogs were circus animals and tried to get them to jump through a hoop and do other tricks. A cat made a great panther peeking out of his cage. Too bad they didn't have any elephants.

Everyone wanted to be an acrobat or a tightrope walker. That box of pink powder made them feel like real performers!

The Herd Is Coming

Alfred's family lived next door to Izzie in town. Izzie and her family lived on Union Street. Towns were different in those days. The streets were not paved and sometimes they were full of mud holes and ruts. The houses were father apart and many people had barns or pens to keep cows. Izzie's family kept two cows. Sometimes they had three.

So many people in Fergus Falls had cows that they hired herdsmen for them. Every morning the herdsmen would come and open the barn doors or gates to the cow pens and the cows would come out, fall into line, and trot off to their pasture outside of town. They stayed there all day with the herdsmen. About five o'clock in the afternoon, the herdsmen would bring them back again.

Each cow knew where she belonged and when the herd passed her gate or barn, she would leave the line and turn in on her own. There were four herds like that in Fergus Falls with about 100 cows in each herd.

When it was time for the cows to come home, Izzie sometimes went to her married sister Tella's house to hear the neighbor's parrot. It sat on its perch on the front porch and when it saw the cows it would shout at the top of its voice, "The herd is coming! The herd is coming!"

You might think it must have been fun to have cows, but it was hard work, too. There were no milking machines in those days, so all those cows had to be milked by hand. Izzie's mother milked their cows. The family kept the milk they needed and sold the rest to families that didn't have their own cows. Izzie and her brother Enoch had to deliver it to them in little covered pails. They sold the milk for six cents a quart.

Sometimes Izzie had other chores to help take care of the cows. In the winter it was her job to take the cows to drink from a stream that didn't freeze over. One cold, sunny day they decided they didn't want to go back home with her.

When they finished their noon drink they just kicked up their heels and romped off to their summer pasture. Izzie was upset because she didn't have time to run all the way out there to catch them. She had to go back to school after lunch. They finally got home on their own, though. They knew the way.

Slates and Sponges

Izzie's school was different from yours in many ways. She never forgot her first day of school. They didn't have kindergarten, so she had never been to school until she started first grade. Her mother told her big brother, Ben, to take her to the first grade room. Ben said, "Sure, I'll do that." But when they got there, Ben just open up the door to the classroom and gave Izzie a great big shove. She landed right in the middle of the room, embarrassed and scared to death. That's a rascally big brother for you.

Once Izzie got used to school, she liked it. They had wooden desks. Tied to each one on a long string was a damp sponge. Can you guess what they were for? They didn't use paper and pencils or pens. They wrote on slates with chalk. It was like each child had his or her own small blackboard. They used the sponges to wipe them off. They thought it was great fun when it was time to wet the sponges.

Their teachers were very strict. They couldn't even whisper to their neighbors. One time, when Izzie's older sister Tella was about twelve years old, their family got a melodian, which is a musical instrument sort of like a piano. Tella was so proud and excited about it that she just had to tell everyone. Since she wasn't allowed to talk, she wrote on her slate, "I got a melodian," and held it up for everyone to see. But her teacher saw it, too, and punished her by hitting her hands with a ruler. Too bad they didn't have "show and tell" in those days.

Tella learned to play the melodian and the organ, too, the kind you pump with your feet. When she was still a teenager, she played the organ in our church. In the winter, it was so cold up in the choir loft that she had to wear her coat and put on her mittens between songs.

At Christmas, she was given a gift of ten dollars for playing the organ every Sunday all year long. She thought she was rich. Ten dollars was a lot of money in those days. I'll bet even the teacher who hit her hands with the ruler was proud of the way she learned to play.

13

This may have been Izzie's School. Taken in about 1874.

Hungry Cows

Children weren't supposed to argue with their teachers. Most of the time, Izzie behaved herself in school and got along fine, but one day she had to argue with her teacher.

In the winter, the cows couldn't go out to the pasture to graze so they had to buy hay for them. One fall, there was an early, unexpected snowstorm and the herdsman had to bring the cows home from the pasture early. Izzie's family had nothing to feed them. It was lunchtime and school would soon be starting again for the afternoon. Izzie was only ten or eleven years old, but her mother told her to ask her teacher if she could be excused from school for a short time to buy hay for the cows.

Izzie's teacher refused to let her go. She insisted she HAD to go, so the teacher told Izzie she would have to go to the principal and ask him. He, too, said, "NO!"

Izzie was so angry she began to cry. She said, "How would you like to be hungry and not have anything to eat?" She cried so hard and felt so sorry for those cows that the principal finally let her go buy the hay. Sometimes those cows sure were trouble!

15

Izzie had her share of trouble with cows. One evening her mother was milking one of them and Izzie was standing next to her brushing the flies away. When her mother was finished milking, the cow decided it was time for trip. Off she went on a trot toward Wessberg's Hill. Izzie's foot got caught in the end of her rope and she was dragged along behind the cow. Izzie screamed so loudly that after a short distance, the cow stopped and turned around to see what all the noise was about. Luckily for Izzie, she stood still while Izzie's mother untangled her foot. Boy, was she scared! She could have been badly hurt if the cow had kept on dragging her, but she just got dirty.

Sunday School All Day Long

Izzie's parents came to America from Norway and they belonged to the Norwegian Lutheran Church. It was on the other side of town from Izzie's house and she didn't know any of the children there. They had to learn to read Bible history and Luther's Catechism in Norwegian. Those are books that taught them about their church's beliefs. Izzie and her friends didn't know how to speak Norwegian so they had to take language lessons first. They started with stuff like "det er cat" and "det er rat." Something about the cat eating the rat, and Izzie didn't like it.

The teacher sat at one end of the pew and the child sitting next to her had to recite the lesson. When that child was finished, he or she was sent to sit at the other end of the pew while the next one read the lesson. Meanwhile, the rest of the class had nothing to do. They just acted like little monkeys, which certainly wasn't what they were supposed to be doing in church.

There were three churches on Izzie's block. She had friends that went to each of them, and that's how she got started going to more than one Sunday school. She went to the Norwegian Lutheran at nine o'clock, the Congregational at noon, and the Baptist or the Norwegian Methodist in the afternoon. My goodness, she should have been a saint!

The Baptist congregation was so small that a woman in Izzie's neighborhood felt sorry for them. She got all of the neighborhood kids together to go to the Baptist Sunday school. She even taught a class for them, although she belonged to the Congregational church.

When Izzie was only about four years old, Alfred's older sister, Anna, wanted to take her to Sunday school. Izzie didn't have a nice, warm coat to wear to church, so Anna found a pretty green coat she had outgrown. It came down almost to Izzie's heels but she wore it anyway. Off they went to the Congregational Sunday school. From then on, Izzie always went with Anna.

Do you wonder why Izzie went to so many different Sunday schools? Actually, it was the best thing to do on Sunday since people weren't allowed to do much else, not even play baseball. People thought it was wrong to do most kinds of work or play because the Commandment says to "keep the Sabbath day holy."

Norwegian Lutheran Church

Toys and Games

Izzie couldn't play on Sunday, but she and her friends had lots of fun playing the rest of the week. They liked to lay out farms. They gathered small, pretty stones and made farms with them by laying them side-by-side in patterns to form fences and the outlines of houses and the rooms in them, like floor plans. They made barns and pastures, too.

They didn't have any little plastic or wooden animals to play with, but they made their own farm animals out of clay, which was really thick mud that they dug up and shaped. They dried the animals in the sun until they baked hard. They played with their clay animals and farms for days at a time. Most of the games they played and the toys they had were things they made or thought up themselves.

21

Every warm evening, all the children in the
neighborhood would gather on Wessberg's Hill to play Blind
Man's Bluff or Run My Good Sheep Run until bedtime.

On the edge of Wessberg's Hill was a large rock. Izzie liked to take her bird dog, Max, and sit on that rock after a storm to watch the clouds form strange shapes. Sometimes they looked like faces, or animals, or mountains. She could imagine them to be almost anything. Max and Izzie also watched the sunsets from that rock.

Izzie liked to climb trees and swing, too. There were several big willow trees in some vacant lots her mother owned next to her sister Tella's house. They had such large, low branches that the children could almost walk right up into them from one limb to another. It was a terrific place to climb. They had swings there, too.

Sometimes they put a long board from one swing to another to make a giant swing. Then they all could swing at once. They liked to put sand on the board. As they swang back and forth, the sand sifted off each side and made lines on the ground. They pretended they were making railroad tracks.

No More Doll

Izzie played with her friend Alfred a lot. Like most kids, they did some pretty silly things. Izzie had a doll with a nicely painted wax face. Dolls in those days had cloth or china bodies and faces made out of wax or china.

Alfred decided that the wax on the doll's face would make good "chewing gum," and he talked Izzie into chewing the wax off the doll's face with him. They had their "gum" all right, but Izzie was awfully sorry afterward.

Another time, Alfred's older sister, Anna, had two very large dolls that were exactly alike. Izzie didn't think it was fair for Anna to have two dolls like that, because she didn't even have one nice, large doll. So, one day, after Izzie played with Anna and her dolls, she just took one of them home with her. She wanted it very badly. Her mother had a hard time getting her to give it back to Anna because Izzie just didn't think Anna had any business having two dolls just alike.

Izzie liked dolls even though she was a tomboy. She liked sewing, too. Judge Baxter lived about a block-and-a-half from her house. His daughter, Bertha, was Izzie's age. Her stepmother started a little club for the neighborhood girls who were Bertha's friends. They met each Saturday afternoon and Mrs. Baxter taught them "fancy work" like sewing and embroidery. After they sewed awhile, Mrs. Baxter served them lunch.

Sometimes she took them to see stage plays in the afternoon. There were no movies, then. The girls sure enjoyed seeing the actors and actresses perform.

Santa From the Ceiling

Christmas was Izzie's favorite time of year. Christmas was always special, with carols and delicious food. Izzie's family always had Norwegian cookies and Christmas bread called Julekage. On Christmas Eve they ate lutefisk and lefse, which are traditional Norwegian foods. Lutefisk is a kind of fish and lefse is a soft, flat bread that might remind you of a flour tortilla.

Their Christmas tree was lovely but dangerous. They didn't have fancy ornaments or electric lights, so they decorated it with paper ornaments, popcorn strung on strings, and real candles. The candles looked so beautiful, but if just one candle had tipped it would have started the tree on fire. Then WHOOSH, the whole tree would have been blazing in a minute. If that had happened, the whole house would have probably burned down. They didn't have good ways to fight fires. Sometimes a family did have a sad Christmas because their home burned from an accident like that. Izzie's family was lucky that they never had a fire.

Izzie enjoyed the Christmas celebrations at all the churches she attended. One time, at the Congregational Church Christmas party, Santa came down a ladder from the attic of the church and gave nuts and candy to all the children. They were thrilled because in those days they didn't get many gifts for Christmas. They got some candy and nuts in their stockings, and maybe an orange if they were lucky. That was a real treat because in those days, oranges in the winter in Minnesota were unusual and expensive. It wasn't like nowadays when you can just go the supermarket and get them any time. They didn't have frozen or canned orange juice, or refrigerators or freezers, either.

When Santa Didn't Come

One Christmas Eve when Izzie went to the Christmas tree program at the Baptist chapel, her brother Enoch came to get her at about nine o'clock. On their way home in the starry night, they heard sleigh bells near a high railroad bridge a few blocks away from their house.

Enoch told Izzie that he knew it was Santa Claus and she'd better hurry home to bed. He said that if Santa saw that she was still up, he wouldn't even stop at their house. Izzie never thought those sleigh bells might have been just someone out for a ride in their sleigh. She ran home as fast as she could.

She was so worried that Santa wouldn't stop that she didn't even finish undressing before she hopped into bed. Of course, Santa did come after she was asleep. He filled her stockings and put some larger presents near her bed.

Izzie's brothers loved to tease her and play tricks on her. One time they wrote a letter and sent it to her. It was supposed to be from Santa Claus and they even signed his name. Izzie was very excited because it said Santa wanted her to come to live with him!

Izzie kept her doll clothes in a cute little trunk of Tella's. She took them out and packed her precious things in it so she'd be all ready when Santa came for her.

She waited for weeks, but of course Santa never did come. She was disappointed for awhile but then she realized she didn't really way to leave her family, and it was cold enough in Minnesota for her. She didn't need the North Pole!

Winter Fun

Sometimes it seemed like they WERE at the North Pole right there in Minnesota. They had lots of snow, so Wessberg's Hill was filled with children on skis, sleds, and bumpers. Izzie's brother, John, even had a toboggan.

"Bumpers" were made by nailing a board upright a little behind the middle of a barrel stave, and then nailing another board on top of that for a seat. A barrel stave is a long, curved board from the side of a wooden barrel. It was like a sled runner or ski. To ride it, you'd sit on the seat and slide down the hill. It was hard to balance and there was no way to steer it, so they took lots of tumbles. You can see a drawing of one at the top of the page.

The Wessbergs had an old cutter. That's a sleigh that was pulled by a horse, like the one in the song, "Jingle Bells." Wessbergs didn't use the cutter any more, so the neighborhood children would climb into it at the top of the hill and down they went. It was like a giant sled, but they couldn't steer it, either. They never knew where it would go, but they didn't worry about that. They were lucky they never got hurt in it.

35

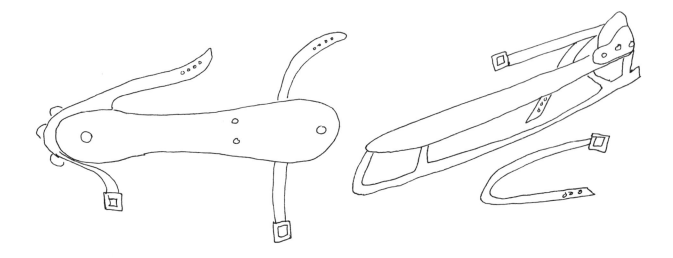

Izzie loved to ice skate, too. She learned on a small pond back of their barn. She didn't have shoe skates. Hers were just blades fastened onto wooden platforms that strapped on over her shoes. When she became a good skater, she went to Lake Alice, a pretty lake right in town.

Izzie liked ice skating so much that sometimes she wasn't as careful as she should have been. Once she got the bright idea to skate across the lake to a friend's house and walk to school with her. She started out across the lake alone. When she was in the middle, she noticed she was on "rubber ice," thin ice that wavers up and down under you. She knew it might break under her and she was terribly frightened, but she didn't dare to stop or turn back. She just kept skating as fast as she could with the ice going up and down all the way. You can be sure she never did that again!

It especially scared her because the year she was born, two boys went under the ice and died. The men in town spent many hours in the cold trying to recover their bodies. Izzie's father was one of those men and he became very ill from the exposure and died. Izzie never knew her father. He died five months before she was born. Her mother took very good care of her and her sister and four brothers, but Izzie wished her father had been there, too.

36

Looking for Pennies

Izzie and her friends liked to look under the sidewalks. They were made of heavy wooden boards laid side-by-side with a narrow space in between. They would crawl along on their hands and knees for a whole block, looking between the boards to see what they could find. They found plenty, but most of it wasn't worth much. If they were lucky, they might find a penny or even a pocket knife. Can you imagine what their clothes looked like after that?

37   A wooden sidewalk in Fergus Falls

Another place they looked for pennies was the church cellar. You think that's a funny place to look for pennies?

Not in Izzie's church. It was a small wooden building. In the cellar, which had a dirt floor, was a boiler from an old threshing machine from someone's farm. It had been converted into a sort of stove to heat the church above.

The floor boards were laid about an inch apart to let the heat come up. Now you can see why Tella's hands were so cold up there in the balcony. Not much heat made it up there.

Some of the children dropped their Sunday school pennies before they were collected and they rolled down between the cracks in the boards. After Sunday school there was always a grand scramble to the basement to look for pennies. It was like a contest to see who could find one. They thought it was the best part of Sunday school.

Izzie and Her Friends and Parents

Izzie had a lot of friends but her best friends were her neighbors, Anna and Alfred Wessberg. Like the other photos in this book (except Izzie's parents below), these pictures of Alfred and Anna were taken in the 1800s. We don't know exactly what year they pictures were taken, or how old Anna and Alfred were at the time. The originals of these photos were "tintypes," an old-fashioned kind of photo on metal.

This is Izzie's parents wedding picture, taken when they were married during the Civil War in 1864. Their names are John and Martha Anderson. This photo was a tintype, too.

Pal and the Valentine Party

Izzie's Sunday school teacher at the Congregational Church was Mrs. Daley. She was such a sweet lady. All the children loved her. She often had parties for the class in her home.

Mrs. Daley had a beautiful, big collie dog named Pal. He was her "errand boy." When she wanted something from town, she wrote a note and put it into a basket. She gave it to Pal and he carried it in his mouth to Mr. Daley, who had a shoe store downtown. Mr. Daley put into the basket whatever his wife had written on the note. Then Pal carried it home to her.

One day, Mrs. Daley had a Valentine party for Izzie's Sunday school class. They had lots of fun playing Drop the Handkerchief; Find the Thimble; Button, Button, Who's Got the Button? and other games.

Suddenly the parlor door opened and in came Pal carrying his basket. It was full of lovely Valentines. Izzie and her friends were surprised and excited. Pal put the basket down in the middle of the floor.

Each child found a fancy, lacy Valentine of her very
own. After they showed them to each other, Mrs. Daley
served white cupcakes with red frosting hearts on them and
hot chocolate.

A Swinging Sheep

Everyone likes to hear this last story about Izzie but hardly anyone wants to try it for themselves. Remember how much Izzie loved to swing? One day she was swinging in her yard and got a big surprise.

Izzie's brothers had a pet sheep. It was cute when it was just a little lamb but when it grew up it was an awful pest. It liked to butt people just like a billy goat.

When Alfred and Izzie were playing and he saw the sheep coming, he would shout, "Lie down flat, Izzie! Lie down flat!" They would both lie down so that old sheep couldn't butt them.

This time, Izzie was swinging high and neither she nor Alfred saw the sheep soon enough. Alfred yelled for Izzie to lie down but it was too late. She couldn't get out of the swing that fast. That old sheep ran up and butted her while she was swinging. He waited until the swing came back down toward him, braced himself, lowered his head, and butted again. He could butt hard and each time he gave Izzie a big boost.

That darned sheep had a hard head and it hurt. All Izzie could do was hang on tight. She kicked and hollered until her mother came and took the sheep away. The whole time, her big brother, Ben, the same one who shoved her into the first grade classroom, was standing in the back doorway laughing at her. He thought it was a big joke.

Nobody ever heard of a sheep swinging someone before. Later, Izzie thought it was fun to tell the story but at the time, she hated it.

Izzie's Family in Fergus Falls

Izzie's family came to Fergus Falls in September 1876. Both her parents were originally from Norway and had lived and married in Dane County, Wisconsin. Her father's first general store was in Marshall, Wisconsin. Later they moved to Calumet, Michigan and then to Fergus Falls where they owned and lived in a house at 204 Union Avenue North. That house is no longer in existence. Izzie's best friends, Anna and Alfred Wessberg lived at 230 Union Avenue North.

When they came, Fergus Falls was a village that was growing fast. In 1875, it had 570 residents, and by 1878 when Izzie was born, it had grown to 680. Izzie's father, John E. Anderson, hoped it would offer a prosperous life for his family. He came ahead of his family, in July 1876, and established a dry goods store on Lincoln Avenue. In February 1877, he moved to another location on Lincoln Avenue, two doors from the bank, and in July 1877, he sold the store to his future son-in-law, Ole Skavlem, who had been working in the store and boarding at his house,. There are numerous advertisements for his store in the newspapers. It is difficult to pinpoint the exact location because the street-numbering system has changed.

On January 1, 1878, two boys went under the ice on Goodsell's Pond on the river. Izzie's father helped in the search for the two boys' bodies and became very ill from the exposure. He had served all four years in the Civil War and contracted tuberculosis while in uniform. He was unable to recover from the illness and died on April 6, 1878, just days short of his 38th birthday. This was the second family tragedy in less than a year. On May 5, 1877, their first daughter named Isabella died at the age of eleven months. Izzie was born on September 24, 1878. In those days, it was common to name another child the same name as a deceased sibling. Both John and his infant daughter are buried in Fergus Falls.

It was interesting to find a newspaper article titled "A Widow in Luck," that publicly noted that Martha Anderson had received $1008.76 in life insurance following John's death. It noted that this would enable the family to have a secure home. Martha ran a boarding house to support her family of six children. A boarding house was a place where people (usually unmarried men) could go to have their meals each day. It was less expensive than eating in a restaurant and offered home cooking and a homey atmosphere.

During the years Izzie lived in Fergus Falls, it grew quickly. In 1880, there were 1,635 residents, and by December 1882 the population was 5,044. By the time she moved away, it was a town of nearly 6,000 people, almost ten times the size it had been twenty years previously, in the year she was born.

Izzie and her family lived in Fergus Falls until 1898. She attended school there through a year of high school. In the 1880s, children's school grades, including grades for "deportment" were published in the newspaper for all to read. Izzie went to the Lutheran Ladies' Seminary in Red Wing, Minnesota in 1897 and 1898.

Izzie as a young woman.

In 1898, she and her mother moved to Stoughton, Wisconsin. Izzie lived there, in a house on the corner of Prairie and Prospect, the rest of her life. She married Helmer Swenson and had two children, Orrin and Dorothy Marion Swenson (Kundiger). She died June 22, 1952 at the age of 73.

Helmer Swenson, Izzie's Husband.

The Authors of "Izzie"

Marion S. Kundiger

Marion Kundiger is Izzie's daughter. She grew up enjoying her mother's stories about her childhood in Fergus Falls, Minnesota, and eventually asked her to write down the incidents in letters. Izzie's letters formed the basis of this book.

When Marion had children of her own, they, too enjoyed Izzie's stories. Marion was convinced she could write a better book than some of those she found to read to her children. Her first version of Izzie was a handmade book illustrated with her watercolors. Children and teachers at a local elementary school received the book well. For over forty years she has hoped to see Izzie in print.

Marion had four children of her own and worked as a medical technologist and biology teacher in high school and at Kansas State University. She is retired, a grandmother of ten and a great-grandmother of three. She lives in Manhattan, Kansas and is a world traveler and photographer. This is her first book.

Jerri Garretson

Jerri Garretson is Marion Kundiger's daughter and Izzie's granddaughter. As a child, she was fascinated with Izzie's stories. She, too, has looked forward to Izzie's publication since the 1950s.

When she started Ravenstone Press in 1997, she knew that Izzie would have to be one of her books. When her oldest son said he hoped to see it for his daughters, she knew it was time to begin.

For this book, Jerri rewrote the text, re-drew the illustrations as ink drawings, and painted the cover illustration.

Jerri chose to publish Izzie in 1998, as Ravenstone Press' second book, to honor her mother on her 80th birthday, and Izzie on her 120th.

Jerri is a children's librarian. She has two grown sons and two granddaughters. She lives with her husband, Peter, in Manhattan, Kansas.

★ Ravenstone Press

P.O. Box 1791, Manhattan KS 66505-1791

Tel: (785) 77~ ~~~~

RETAIL MAIL ORDER ~~~~

Izzie: Growing Up on the Plains in the ~~~~
bookstore or historical society. If not, orde~~~~
plus shipping (plus Kansas tax for address~~~~
table below. Shipping and handling = $2.0(~~~~
additional book.

DISCOUNTS, DELIVERIES & PROGR~~~~
over 5 books, or for commercial resale, scho~~~~
Manhattan, Kansas area may be arranged~~~~
present programs.

Please enclose payment (check or mor~~~~
Ravenstone Press
(Sorry, credit card orders are not accepted.~~~~

Mail order to:
Ravenstone Press - Orders
P.O. Box 1791
Manhattan KS 66505-1791

Total Mail Order Price (Kansas addresses~~~~
1 book = $ 8.50
2 books = $ 15.66
3 books = $ 22.82
4 books = $ 29.99
5 books = $ 37.15

5-6

DIVISION OF EDUCATION
KANSAS MUSEUM OF HISTORY
6425 SW 6TH AVENUE
TOPEKA KS 66615-1099

QUANTITY ORDERED (Kansas Addresses)	TOTAL DUE (Includes Books, Shipping & Tax)

QUANTITY ORDERED (Out-of-State Addresses)	TOTAL DUE (Includes Books & Shipping)

Ship Order To:

Name:_____

Street Address:_____

City:_____

State & Zip Code:_____

Tel:_____